A New True Book

THE RUSSIAN FEDERATION

By Karen Jacobsen

CHILDRENS PRESS®

CHICAGO

Little girls looking in a window at
the GUM department store in Moscow

PHOTO CREDITS

AP/Wide World Photos–27 (right), 28, 33, 34, 39, 43 (right)

The Bettmann Archive–22 (right), 25, 29, 32

GeoIMAGERY–© Al Jorolan, Cover

© Virginia R. Grimes–5 (2 photos), 23, 45

H. Armstrong Roberts–24, 30 (2 photos); © G. Roessler, 2

North Wind Picture Archives–20 (right), 22 (left)

Photri–11 (2 photos), 12, 13 (left), 36 (right), 37, 41 (2 photos); © Mark Wadlow, 44 (left)

Reuters/Bettmann–43 (left)

Bob & Ira Spring–17

Tom Stack & Associates–© Jack Stein Grove, 15

Stock Montage–19, 20 (left), 27 (left)

SuperStock International, Inc.– © W. Beerman, 6

UPI/Bettmann–36 (left)

Valan–© Fred Bremmer, 7

Reprinted with permission of *The New Book of Knowledge*, © Grolier Inc.–4

Map by Len Meents–10

COVER: Nursery school children

Project Editor: Fran Dyra
Design: Margrit Fiddle

Library of Congress Cataloging-in-Publication Data

Jacobsen, Karen
    The Russian Federation / by Karen Jacobsen.
       p.   cm.–(A New true book)
    Includes index.
    ISBN 0-516-01060-3
    1.   Russia (Federation)–Juvenile literature.
[1.   Russia (Federation).]   I.   Title.
DK510.56.J33   1994
947–dc20   93-36996
                                                            CIP
                                                            AC

TABLE OF CONTENTS

Russia is one state in the Commonwealth of Independent States.

THE NATION

The Russian Federation, or Russia, is the world's largest nation. It stretches for more than 6 million square miles (15.5 million square kilometers) across eastern Europe and northern Asia.

4

Russians in traditional costume playing and singing (left)
and a Russian father and son in St. Petersburg

Almost 150 million
people live in Russia. Most
Russians are Slavs, though
there are several other
ethnic groups. Dozens of
languages are spoken in
the nation, but the official
language is Russian.

The Russian Federation
is a democracy with a

Moscow, Russia's capital city, lies along the Moscow River.
It has a population of about 9 million.

constitution. The people elect a president and a parliament, which makes the nation's laws. The Russian Federation has 31 self-governing republics and regions. Moscow is the nation's capital.

6

THE LAND

Russia has three very different land and climate areas—tundra, taiga, and steppe. They spread across this vast nation in wide bands.

The flat and frozen tundra lies in the far north,

These trees are growing at the treeline, the boundary between the taiga forest and the tundra.

near the Arctic Ocean.
There are no trees. Only
short grasses, mosses,
and hardy lichen plants
grow on the tundra.
Temperatures in this area
are well below 0°F (−18°C)
during much of the year.
Summers are short and
cool.

The taiga, a tree-
covered, swampy area, lies
south of the tundra. Most
taiga trees are needle-leaf
evergreens.

The steppe is a broad plain covered with short grasses.

The steppe–a flat, grass-covered plain–is south of the taiga. On the steppe, the summers are warm and last long enough for crops to grow.

9

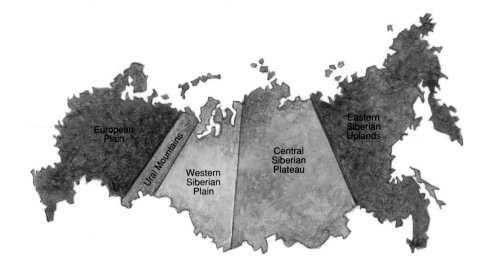

FIVE REGIONS

Russia has five geographic regions: the European Plain, the Ural Mountains, the Western Siberian Plain, the Central Siberian Plateau, and the Eastern Siberian Uplands. Wide bands of tundra and taiga stretch across all five regions.

A forest in the taiga section of eastern Russia (left) and a traditional wooden house in the city of Irkutsk, Siberia.

Most of Russia's people live on the European Plain. The steppe of the European Plain has some of the nation's best farmland. The taiga forests provide wood for houses, ships, and fuel.

11

The Volga River near the city of Gorky. The river provides
water transportation for a huge area in western Russia.

Many streams and rivers
flow through the European
Plain. The Volga, Europe's
longest river, is the most
important. It flows south for
2,142 miles (3,447 kilometers)
into the Caspian Sea.

Russia's beautiful mountains: A swiftly moving stream in the Caucasus (left) and a scenic view of the Urals.

The Caucasus Mountains rise between the Caspian and Black seas. They mark the southern edge of the European Plain.

The Ural Mountains are low and rounded. They

13

separate the European Plain from the Western Siberian Plain.

Tundra and taiga cover the north of the Western Siberian Plain. In the south, wide, grassy steppes provide grazing land for large herds of cattle.

The Central Siberian Plateau lies east of the Western Siberian Plain. It is a major uranium- and

A view of the Siberian mining town of Komsomolsk

tin-mining area. The Lena River divides Central and Eastern Siberia.

The Eastern Siberian Uplands is a wild region of tundra and taiga. High mountains and plateaus line the long Pacific coast.

LONG AGO IN RUSSIA

In the A.D. 600s, groups
of Slavs from central
Europe began to move
east on the European
Plain. They settled along
riverbanks and in forest
lands. Later, in the 800s,
Vikings from Scandinavia
sailed down the rivers.
They attacked the Slavs.
What they did not steal,
they burned.

In 862 a group of
Vikings known as the Rus

Ancient churches in the city of Novgorod

set up a trading center in
Novgorod. The Rus were
the first rulers in the land
that became known as
Russia. The Rus built cities.
The greatest was Kiev in
what is now Ukraine.

17

Vladimir I, a Rus prince, ruled Kiev. In A.D. 988, he became a Christian and joined the Greek Orthodox church. Vladimir I made the people become Orthodox Christians. He also introduced an alphabet and brought reading and writing to the Russian people.

In 1237, Mongol troops invaded Russia from the east. The Mongols ruled

parts of European Russia
for more than 200 years.

In 1462, an army of
Russian Slavs defeated the
Mongols and took over the
land around Moscow. Their

This scene shows the Russian army of Ivan III,
equipped with horses and armor, defeating the Mongols
with their camels and curved swords.

Left: Ivan III ruled Russia from 1462 to 1505.
Right: Ivan IV ruled from 1533 to 1584. His many cruel
acts earned him the name Ivan the Terrible.

leader became Ivan III—the
first ruler to call himself
"tsar of the Russians." *Tsar*
is the Russian word for
"caesar," or "ruler."

Ivan IV—known as Ivan
the Terrible—became tsar in

1533. Ivan IV was a cruel ruler. He took land from its rightful owners and gave it to his followers. Ivan IV then passed a law that made the peasants into serfs. The people who lived and worked on the land thus became the property of the landowners.

THE ROMANOVS

In 1613, Russian leaders chose Michael Romanov, a sixteen-year-old boy, to be the new tsar. The Romanov family ruled Russia for the next 300 years.

Michael's grandson Peter became tsar In 1689. He was known as Peter the Great. Peter made Russia

The Naval Institute in St. Petersburg was founded by Peter the Great. He wanted to have a modern navy like the Western European nations.

into a modern European nation. He built ships and created a strong Russian navy. He also built factories and schools.

In 1703, Tsar Peter started to build a new capital near the Baltic Sea— St. Petersburg.

THE GROWTH OF EMPIRE

Catherine II is known as Catherine the Great. She was a German princess who was married to Tsar Peter III and became the ruler of the Russian Empire after his death.

From 1762 to 1796, a tsarina–Catherine II–ruled the Russian Empire. She made St. Petersburg a world center for the arts and education. Her army captured land from Poland

A painting of Napoleon's army retreating from Russia. The army of 600,000 lost more than 500,000 men in the difficult winter conditions.

and from the Ottoman Empire (now Turkey).

In 1812, Napoleon, the emperor of France, and his powerful army invaded Russia. They got as far as Moscow before the cold Russian winter forced them to retreat. At the end of the war, Russia controlled even more land.

In 1861, Tsar Alexander II decided to improve the lives of his people. He set up local governments. He freed the serfs and gave them small plots of land.

But many Russians wanted more changes. They wanted a leader elected by the people. They wanted to get rid of the tsar. In 1881, a terrorist bomb killed Alexander II.

In 1894, Nicholas II became tsar. By that time, the Russian Empire

Tsar Alexander II (left) was killed by terrorists in spite of his reforms. Nicholas II (right) was the last Romanov to rule Russia.

reached all the way to the Pacific Ocean. It was costly and difficult to control so much land.

To make matters worse, the harvest failed. Food shortages made life hard for the Russian people.

Soldiers gather in St. Petersburg to march off to
fight against Germany in World War I.

In 1914, Russia entered
World War I on the side of
Great Britain and France.
Millions of Russian soldiers
were killed or wounded.
Nicholas II became more
unpopular than ever.

LENIN AND THE RUSSIAN REVOLUTION

In March 1917, the people rebelled against Nicholas II. Riots and strikes grew violent. Battles raged in Moscow and St. Petersburg. By October,

The tsar's troops used machine guns to fight rebels in St. Petersburg.

Tsar Nicholas II gave up his throne in 1917. The Bolsheviks, led by V. I. Lenin (right), held Tsar Nicholas II as a prisoner in Siberia (left).

the Bolshevik (Communist) party was in power. Their leader was V. I. Lenin. Tsar Nicholas II and his family were held as prisoners.

Lenin signed a peace treaty with Germany in

March 1918. But, inside Russia, civil war broke out between the Communists—the Reds—and the anti-Communists—the Whites. The Whites wanted to stop Lenin and choose a new leader for Russia.

In 1920, Lenin and the Communists won the civil war. In 1922, they formed a new government and gave the Russian Empire a new name—the Union of Soviet Socialist Republics (USSR), or the Soviet Union.

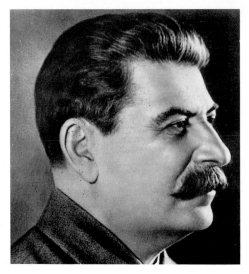

THE SOVIET UNION

Joseph Stalin took over as leader of the Soviet Union after Lenin's death.

In 1924, Lenin died and Joseph Stalin took over. Stalin set up Five-Year Plans to modernize farming and industry in the Soviet Union. But he became a cruel leader with more power than a tsar. Under Stalin's rule millions of Russian people were killed or sent to prison in Siberia.

These German soldiers were captured by the Russian army at the great battle in the city of Stalingrad during World War II.

In 1941, the German army invaded the Soviet Union. Millions of people died in the war. Finally, the Soviet army drove the Germans back into Germany—and to defeat.

After World War II ended in 1945, the Soviet Union

The people of Hungary rebelled against the control of the Soviet Union in 1956. These Hungarian freedom fighters are battling Russian troops.

took over the Baltic nations of Estonia, Latvia, and Lithuania. Several other European nations— East Germany, Poland, Czechoslovakia, Hungary, Romania, Yugoslavia, and Bulgaria—also came under Soviet Communist control.

THE COLD WAR

During the 1950s, 1960s,
and 1970s, the Soviet
Union and the United
States were enemies.

They fought a "Cold War,"
with spies and threats.
They kept huge armies
and built dangerous
weapons. Many times the
two superpowers came
very close to turning the
Cold War into a "hot war."

The United States and

The Russian cosmonaut Yuri Gagarin was the first human to travel into space. *Sputnik 1* (right) was the world's first artificial satellite.

the Soviet Union also competed in the exploration of space. The Soviets had many successes.

On October 4, 1957, their *Sputnik 1* became the first artificial satellite to orbit the Earth. On April 12, 1961, Soviet cosmonaut Yuri Gagarin became the first man in space.

Mikhail Gorbachev was the last leader of the Soviet Union before the union broke apart in 1991.

THE END OF THE SOVIET UNION

In 1985, Mikhail Gorbachev became the new leader of the Soviet Union. The nation had many problems. Communism was not working. Gorbachev started to make changes to improve life for his people. He made peace with the United States. He gave more freedom to the Soviet Union's fifteen republics. In 1989, the republics had their first free elections.

By December 1991, the fifteen republics had voted to become independent nations. Gorbachev resigned from office. The Soviet Union no longer existed.

Eleven of the former

	RUSSIA *Moscow		TURKMENISTAN *Ashkhabad
	KYRGYZSTAN *Bishkek		KAZAKHSTAN *Alma-Ata
AZERBAIJAN *Baku	MOLDOVA *Kishinev	UKRAINE *Kiev	TAJIKISTAN *Dashanbe
ARMENIA *Yerevan	BELARUS *Minsk	UZBEKISTAN *Tashkent	

Above: The Commonwealth of Independent States and their capital cities. Right: Russian cosmonaut Sergei Krikalev stayed in orbit for ten months. When he returned to Earth in March 1992, his country—the Soviet Union— no longer existed.

Soviet republics formed the Commonwealth of Independent States (CIS). Its role is to solve problems and keep peace among the member nations.

39

THE NEW NATION

Today, the leaders of the Russian Federation are still writing its laws. There are many quarrels between ethnic groups. Siberian Russia doesn't trust European Russia. Some republics want to leave the federation and become independent nations. No one knows for sure if the Russian Federation will hold together or split up into several smaller nations.

Russian preschool children studying English (left). Russian students study a wide variety of subjects. They work hard and place a high value on their education.

LIFE IN THE RUSSIAN FEDERATION

Students in Russia attend free public schools for eleven years. Some students in the ninth through eleventh grades attend special schools that prepare them for jobs.

41

They may take courses in engineering, agriculture, or industry.

Other students attend general secondary schools. They prepare to study advanced sciences or languages in a university.

In old Russia, Christian holy days such as Christmas and Easter were very important. But the Communist government of the Soviet Union did not approve of religion or religious holidays. Today,

Freedom of religion has returned to Russia. Russian Orthodox priests (above) hold the first service in seventy years in Moscow's St. Basil's Cathedral, and a Christmas tree (right) is displayed in the GUM department store.

the Russian Federation allows freedom of religion for all faiths.

Russia supports its fine athletes. They compete in swimming and diving, skating, skiing, gymnastics, and track-and-field. Soccer

Chess (left) is played by people throughout the Russian Federation. This huge skating rink (right) is used to train skaters for the Olympic Games.

is the nation's most popular sport, but ice hockey is also a favorite.

Many Russian families enjoy hiking or camping on summer vacations. And Russians of all ages love to play chess.

The Russian Federation is a nation of rich natural

Shoppers crowd a main street in St. Petersburg, the city that was built by Peter the Great for his new capital.

resources and great beauty. Its people are proud, strong, and clever. For centuries, their lives have been filled with hardship and trouble. But today they have a new democracy–a chance to create a future of peace and prosperity.

WORDS YOU SHOULD KNOW

artificial (ar • tih • FISH • il)—made by people; not natural

civil war (SIV • il WOR)—a war between different groups within a
country

Communists (KAH • myoo • nists)—people who believe in a system
of government under which businesses are owned by
the state

constitution (KAHN • stih • too • shun)—a set of rules or laws for the
government of a nation

cosmonaut (KAHZ • muh • nawt)—the Russian term for a person
who travels in space

democracy (dih • MAH • kruh • see)—rule by the people or by
representatives of the people

ethnic group (ETH • nik GROOP)—a people with a common
language, customs, and history

exploration (ex • plor • RAY • shun)—traveling to a place to find out
what is there

federation (fed • er • RAY • shun)—a union of several states

independent (in • dih • PEN • dint)—free from the control of another
country or person

lichen (LIKE • in)—a plant made up of a small green plant, called an
alga, and a fungus living together

parliament (PAR • la • mint)—an elected group that represents the
people and makes laws for a country

plain (PLANE)—a large, nearly flat piece of land

plateau (plah • TOH)—an area of elevated flat land

rebel (rih • BEL)—to rise up against authority

republic (rih • PUB • lik)—a country with elected leaders

resources (REE • sore • sez)—natural supplies of such materials as
oil, gas, wood, or minerals

retreat (rih • TREET)—to go back; to break off a battle

satellite (SAT • ih • lite)—a body, such as a moon, that revolves
around a planet

serfs (SERFS)—agricultural workers who are not free to leave the land

steppe (STEP)—a grass-covered plain

taiga (TYE • gah)—the area of evergreen forest south of the tundra

terrorist (TAIR • uh • rist)—a person who uses violent tactics to promote a cause

treaty (TREE • tee)—a written agreement between two groups, having to do with trade, peace, etc.

tsar (ZAR)—the ruler of the Russian Empire before the Russian Revolution of 1917

tundra (TUN • dra)—a cold, treeless area where the vegetation consists of short grasses, mosses, and lichens

university (yoo • nih • VER • sih • tee)—a college or other school of higher learning

uranium (yoo • RAIN • ee • um)—a mineral that is used to make fuel for nuclear power plants

Vikings (VYE • kingz)—Scandinavian people who were pirates and raiders

INDEX

About the Author

Karen Jacobsen is a graduate of the University of Connecticut and Syracuse University. She has been a teacher and is a writer. She likes to find out about interesting subjects and then write about them.